SUMMARY & ANALYSIS

OF

CHRIS BEAT CANCER

A COMPREHENSIVE PLAN FOR HEALING NATURALLY

A GUIDE TO THE BOOK BY CHRIS WARK

NOTE: This book is a summary and analysis and is meant as a companion to, not a replacement for, the original book.

Please follow this link to purchase a copy of the original book: **https://amzn.to/2SexvyK**

Copyright © 2018 by ZIP Reads. All rights reserved. This book or parts thereof may not be reproduced in any form, stored in any retrieval system, or transmitted in any form by any means—electronic, mechanical, photocopy, recording, or otherwise—without prior written permission of the publisher, except as provided by United States of America copyright law. This book is intended as a companion to, not a replacement for the original book. ZIP Reads is wholly responsible for this content and is not associated with the original author in any way.

TABLE OF CONTENTS

SYNOPSIS **6**

CHAPTER 1: INTO THE JUNGLE **7**

Key Takeaway: You never have as much control over your life as you think. 7

Key Takeaway: In times of trouble, your faith in God makes a difference. 8

Key Takeaway: Despite what most people believe, conventional medicine doesn't have all the answers. 9

CHAPTER 2: SURVIVAL OF THE SICKEST **10**

Key Takeaway: Cancer is a modern disease that will never have one cure. 10

Key Takeaway: You are not as healthy as you think. 11

Key Takeaway: Cancer can be contagious 12

CHAPTER 3: DOCTOR'S ORDERS **13**

Key Takeaway: Doctors are not saints. 13

Key Takeaway: Medical treatment kills thousands every year. 14

Key Takeaway: Doctors use medical terminologies to confuse patients. 14

CHAPTER 4: MAKING A KILLING **16**

Key Takeaway: The medical-industrial complex controls every aspect of healthcare. 16

Key Takeaway: America is a drug-dependent nation. 17

CHAPTER 5: IT'S NOT LIKE I NEED YOUR BUSINESS **18**

Key Takeaway: Oncology is a business rather than a humanitarian mission. 18

Key Takeaway: Drug companies manipulate the FDA to approve their drugs. 19

CHAPTER 6: THE ELEPHANT IN THE WAITING ROOM 20

Key Takeaway: Despite public pronouncements, the cancer death rate has not significantly improved. 20
Key Takeaway: Reduction in smoking is the biggest reason for the improvement in cancer deaths. 21
Key Takeaway: Cancer data is often biased to favor drug companies. 21

CHAPTER 7: THE BEAT CANCER MINDSET 23

Key Takeaway: You are responsible for your cancer. 23
Key Takeaway: Be willing to make sacrifices. 23
Key Takeaway: Take consistent, radical action. 24
Key Takeaway: Don't be afraid to make future plans. 24
Key Takeaway: Don't forget to enjoy life. 25

CHAPTER 8: PLANTS VERSUS ZOMBIES 26

Key Takeaway: Berries and lemons are the best anticancer fruits. 26
Key Takeaway: Vegetables from the allium and cruciferous family are potent cancer killers. 27
Key Takeaway: Turmeric, oregano, and cayenne pepper are the best anticancer spices. 27
Key Takeaway: Some herbal teas are better at fighting cancer than others. 28

CHAPTER 9: HEROIC DOSES 29

Key Takeaway: Plants are the key to beating cancer. 29
Key Takeaway: Juicing is better than chewing food. 30
Key Takeaway: Fermented foods are good for your gut bacteria. 30

CHAPTER 10: BUILDING A NEW BODY 32

Key Takeaway: Moving closer to nature can help you beat cancer. 32
Key Takeaway: Your poop indicates how healthy your body is. 33

CHAPTER 11: TAKE OUT THE TRASH 34

Key Takeaway: Always check the label before buying. 34
Key Takeaway: Avoid foods and products containing mercury and aluminum. 34
Key Takeaway: Clean up your air and your airwaves. 35
Key Takeaway: You pay a heavy price for maintaining your beauty. 36

CHAPTER 12: LET'S GET PHYSICAL 38

Key Takeaway: Too much exercise is bad for your health. 38
Key Takeaway: Jumping on a trampoline helps your lymphatic system detoxify your body. 39
Key Takeaway: The sun can protect you from cancer. 39

CHAPTER 13: UNDER PRESSURE 41

Key Takeaway: Stress deactivates your immune system. 41
Key Takeaway: Stress is a good thing, but chronic stress is a killer. 42
Key Takeaway: Be proactive in relieving stress. 43

CHAPTER 14: SPIRITUAL HEALING 44

Key Takeaway: You must think positively to beat cancer. 44
Key Takeaway: Put your faith in God. 45
Key Takeaway: Guard your heart against bitterness and resentment. 45

EDITORIAL REVIEW 46
BACKGROUND ON AUTHOR 49

SYNOPSIS

In his book *Chris Beat Cancer*, Chris Wark shares how he defied conventional medicine and beat cancer using nutritional therapy and lifestyle change. He believes that chemotherapy is not the best option and cancer patients should seriously consider naturopathic treatments.

When you are young and successful, you rarely take note of your health. Chris contends that he was too busy living the fast life to notice that he was neglecting his body. After being diagnosed with colorectal cancer at 26 years of age, he was devastated. At first, he follows the conventional route and undergoes stomach surgery. However, a series of events cause him to lose faith in conventional medicine. His instincts tell him that chemotherapy is more harmful than beneficial, and after some research, he decides not to go through with it.

Instead, he chooses to heal his body by radically transforming his diet and lifestyle. His family and doctors try to convince him otherwise, but Chris is adamant. He adopts a raw-food, plant-based diet and puts his faith in God.

Chris Beat Cancer is a reminder that conventional medicine doesn't have all the answers. God created the human body to heal itself of any disease so long as you eliminate all the toxins from your diet and lifestyle. The medical fraternity knows that chemotherapy doesn't work but is unwilling to speak the truth about cancer, just so that they can keep making a profit.

CHAPTER 1: INTO THE JUNGLE

Wark describes how his dream start to life and marriage was shattered by a cancer diagnosis. At just 26 years of age, Wark leaves his dead-end financial planning job to start his own real estate company. Everything is going great except for the periodic and terrible stomach pains. His wife convinces him to visit a doctor, and he is diagnosed with colorectal cancer. Their faith in God keeps them going.

At first, Wark decides to follow the conventional route of surgery followed by chemotherapy. But through a series of divinely-inspired events, he changes his mind and chooses an alternative solution. He decides to fight cancer by radically changing his diet and lifestyle. Very few people support his decision, and though he is terrified of making the wrong choice, Wark decides to abandon conventional medicine. He ultimately gains support from others who believe that the best way to beat cancer is through nutrition. To this day, he is cancer-free.

Key Takeaway: You never have as much control over your life as you think.

Prior to his cancer diagnosis, Wark was a successful real estate investor who owned more than 30 rental properties. He was part of a band and had even been interviewed for a spot on *The Apprentice*. Wark contends that when life is good, it's easy to feel in control of your circumstances. But after the diagnosis, he realizes that he never really had any control over his life. He concludes that cancer has opened his eyes to what is really important in life—good health and loving relationships.

Key Takeaway: In times of trouble, your faith in God makes a difference.

As Christians, Wark and his wife, Micah, rely on Jesus to strengthen them during their dark moments. Wark believes that God continually brought people into his life to reaffirm his faith and show him the path to follow. The nurse who admitted him had a Psalm 23 note pinned on her cubicle, and reading it before surgery encouraged him immensely. Wark claims that he had a sense of peace in his heart because he trusted God no matter the outcome.

Another divine intervention occurred when Wark receives a book from one of his father's acquaintances. In the book, the author describes how he of opted out of surgery and chemotherapy and chose to eat a raw-food diet. Within one year, his colon cancer was gone. When at the oncologist's office, he watches a TV show where Jack LaLanne talks about how eating fruits and vegetables can heal the body of any disease. Wark contends that all these are signs from God to avoid conventional medicine and have faith that his body can heal itself naturally.

Key Takeaway: Despite what most people believe, conventional medicine doesn't have all the answers.

After his surgery, Wark accepts to follow everything the doctor says. But certain events make him reconsider. The first one is the meal he was served after surgery. Wark states that he expected a healthy meal but was given a sloppy joe instead. Later on, the doctor surprises him by saying that he shouldn't bother with eating healthy foods to heal his weakened body.

Wark also begins to wonder whether the pain medication he is taking is doing him more harm than good. Years later, he discovers that opioid-based painkillers actually trigger cancer and are highly addictive. Though his instincts tell him that chemotherapy is a bad idea, his family thinks he is crazy and pressures him to follow the doctor's recommendations. When the oncologist turns out to be a cold and impersonal man who disparages him, he begins to doubt whether his doctors are telling him the truth. Since Wark believes that God is presenting him with an alternative path, he ignores chemo and transforms his diet instead.

CHAPTER 2: SURVIVAL OF THE SICKEST

Wark provides ample evidence to suggest that the modern lifestyle and environment are responsible for the explosion of cancers all over America. Though humanity has benefitted from industrialization, it has also led to an increase in toxins in the air, food, water, and soil. On top of that, most of the products you use daily contain carcinogenic chemicals that have not been tested for safety.

Wark contends that the Western diet, an inactive lifestyle, and harmful chemicals are making people sicker every day. Statistics show that 70 percent of the preventable deaths in the USA are caused by tobacco use, lack of exercise, and poor nutrition. Research also shows that lifestyle, diet, and environmental factors are responsible for 90 percent of cancer cases.

Key Takeaway: Cancer is a modern disease that will never have one cure.

Research shows that cancer was extremely rare throughout history. Wark states that out of 1,000 mummies, only five have been found to have tumors. It wasn't until the Industrial Revolution in the 1600s that scientists began documenting rising incidences of different forms of cancer. The great innovations of industrialization have also led to massive pollution of the environment, which coincides with the cancer epidemic. According to Wark, this suggests that cancer is a modern phenomenon.

Wark also argues that cancer is not just one disease, but actually refers to "a broad array of unique diseases…that lead to uncontrolled cell growth." Therefore, it is impossible for cancer to ever have one singular cure.

Key Takeaway: You are not as healthy as you think.

Wark states that less than three percent of Americans are living a healthy lifestyle. The marketing industry has convinced many Americans that the food they eat is healthy, but in reality, it is not. A healthy lifestyle must include:

- Regular exercise
- Not smoking
- Not being obese
- Five daily servings of vegetables and fruits

However, very few Americans meet these four conditions. The American diet comprises of highly processed grains, sugars, processed fats, and animal products. Most Americans are also overweight and rarely get any kind of exercise. Wark argues that most people are eating all the necessary macronutrients, but very few actually consume enough micronutrients like minerals and antioxidants. Yet it is these micronutrients that help fight cancer.

Key Takeaway: Cancer can be contagious

Research shows that some viral infections increase the risk of developing cancer, with 20 percent of cancers being caused by such viruses. Some of these viral infections include:

- Hepatitis B and C
- HIV
- Human Papilloma Virus
- Bovine leukemia virus
- Kaposi sarcoma herpes
- Congenital Cytomegalovirus

Though some of these viruses are difficult to avoid, you can control them by making the right lifestyle and dietary choices. Wark states that maintaining a healthy immune system is the best defense against infections.

CHAPTER 3: DOCTOR'S ORDERS

Wark claims that the healthcare industry is killing more people than it is curing. Treating diseases is big business, and many doctors tend to overdiagnose and overtreat patients just to generate cash. Studies show that millions of cancer patients die from unnecessary treatments caused by radiation therapy and drug reactions.

Doctors also use fear to force patients to quickly accept chemotherapy, thus preventing patients from taking the time to consider alternative treatments. Wark contends that the cancer industry isn't being honest with its failures. Simply put, the Hippocratic principle to "First, do no harm" is no longer being practiced.

Key Takeaway: Doctors are not saints.

Just because someone has earned a medical degree doesn't mean they automatically become moral or ethical. Wark argues that some doctors are in it only for the money, such as Dr. Farid Fata, who falsely diagnosed hundreds of patients just to receive millions of dollars in Medicare payments. Doctors are not superhuman and they also succumb to pressure. This explains why doctors have a higher suicide rate than the rest of the population.

Key Takeaway: Medical treatment kills thousands every year.

Research shows that medical treatment (iatrogenesis) is the third leading killer in America. More than 250,000 people die annually due to prescription drug reactions, hospital-acquired infections, surgical errors, medication errors, and unnecessary surgery.

Wark contends that these numbers are inaccurately low because most doctors are trained not to admit liability if they unintentionally kill patients. For example, instead of admitting that a patient died from chemotoxicity, they simply write "heart failure" as the cause of death.

Key Takeaway: Doctors use medical terminologies to confuse patients.

Wark states that most cancer patients believe chemotherapy is a curative treatment, yet it is only a form of palliative care that buys you more time. Doctors use medical jargon to deliberately confuse patients so that they keep coming back for more treatment.

Some of the terminologies used and their actual meanings include:

- This type of cancer responds favorably to (name of drug)/Your cancer is in remission – The drug causes cancer cells to reduce in number temporarily but the tumor will grow again more aggressively.

- These drugs increase overall survival – Patients who took the drugs survived for a few more months before dying

Wark argues that statements like these give patients hope of a total cure, yet the doctors refuse to acknowledge that the benefits are only temporary.

CHAPTER 4: MAKING A KILLING

According to Wark, pharmaceutical companies are purely driven by profit. They make billions of dollars annually thanks to their overwhelming influence over doctors and politicians in America. This has turned America into a medicated nation. Worse still, most of the evidence that is used to justify the development of cancer drugs has been found to be fabricated.

Yet drug companies continue to ignore effective nutrition-based treatments like diet, exercise, and lifestyle changes because they can't legally patent such things. If it's not profitable, they won't touch it, even if it will save lives.

Key Takeaway: The medical-industrial complex controls every aspect of healthcare.

Wark states that the pharmaceutical industry has unrivaled influence over medicine, and sometimes, even politics. Drug companies give funding to medical schools, the American Medical Association, and the Food and Drug Administration. More than 1,200 lobbyists in Washington are on the payroll of drug companies and they often finance the campaigns of politicians. The Bush administration even passed legislation to allow pharmaceutical companies to charge whatever prices they wanted.

Key Takeaway: America is a drug-dependent nation.

Research shows that 50 percent of Americans are taking at least one prescription drug per month. Yet prescription drugs have numerous side effects and are extremely addictive, with the number of overdoses quadrupling between 1990 and 2010.

Wark argues that prescription drugs kill more than 100,000 people annually, with more people dying from opioid painkillers like hydrocodone and oxycodone than heroin and cocaine combined. Pharmaceutical companies have convinced Americans that prescription pills are completely necessary despite their deadly side effects.

CHAPTER 5:
IT'S NOT LIKE I NEED YOUR BUSINESS

When doctors discovered that mustard gas caused body cells to die, they began testing the toxic agent on cancer patients. This marked the invention of chemotherapy. According to Wark, cancer is such big business that oncologists, pharmaceutical companies, and even the FDA often compromise public safety for profit.

Cancer treatments don't just destroy your health; they are financially crippling. New cancer drugs are more expensive than ever, yet they aren't more effective than those of a cheaper variety. One study showed that if oncologists are paid a flat rate per patient instead of per drug, the cost of cancer treatments would fall by 34 percent. Another study revealed that cancer patients are 2.5 times more likely to declare bankruptcy than anybody else. Most patients give up after spending their last dime with no cure in sight.

Key Takeaway: Oncology is a business rather than a humanitarian mission.

Out of all the different branches of medicine, oncology is the one that is mostly run as a business. Cancer drugs generate the most sales in America, second only to heart disease medication. You can't just walk into a pharmacy and buy cancer drugs. They are only available at oncology clinics, which buy them wholesale from manufacturers and then slap a high margin on them. This is why 67 percent of the income made by private oncologists comes from chemo drugs. According to Wark "Treating cancer is not a humanitarian pursuit; it is a billion-dollar business."

Key Takeaway: Drug companies manipulate the FDA to approve their drugs.

The role of the FDA is to ensure that food and drugs are safe for consumption, and manufacturers don't make false claims on their products. However, the FDA is being influenced by drug companies to approve new drugs that are often harmful to users.

Wark states that drug companies pay the FDA a "user fee" of $2.1 million for every drug submitted for approval. They also plant people in FDA approval panels. In one instance, an entire panel was paid by a drug company to approve a new medication. By the time a drug is found to be defective and recalled, the company has already recouped its investment and then some.

CHAPTER 6:
THE ELEPHANT IN THE WAITING ROOM

The cancer industry is very vocal in touting its achievements in fighting cancer. But Wark argues that their data is biased, and they often take credit they don't deserve just to make more profits. The cancer industry is spinning the statistics to cover up the fact that conventional cancer treatments aren't working. Though Wark is critical of the cancer industry, he claims that he is simply trying to enlighten people so that they make more informed decisions.

Key Takeaway: Despite public pronouncements, the cancer death rate has not significantly improved.

In the early years of the 20th century, the cancer death rate was 1 in 500 Americans. By 1991, it had peaked at 215 deaths in every 100,000 people. Today, that number has dropped to about 1 in 537 annually. Though the cancer industry celebrates this as a significant achievement, Wark argues that this only represents a five percent improvement. There has been no progress in reducing the survival rate of epithelial cancers, which comprise 80 percent of all cancer cases.

Key Takeaway: Reduction in smoking is the biggest reason for the improvement in cancer deaths.

In 2016, a report was released stating that cancer deaths had reduced by 23 percent since 1991. The media was told that this was due to early screening, detection, and better treatments. However, Wark claims that this is a misrepresentation of facts. The primary cause for this drop was the reduction in the smoking of cigarettes. Smoking is the leading cause of cancer, and research suggests that less smoking between 1991 and 2003 led to a 40 percent drop in cancer deaths in men. But for some reason, the cancer industry would rather give credit to their cancer treatments.

Key Takeaway: Cancer data is often biased to favor drug companies.

Data from the National Cancer Institute suggests that since 1975, there has been a 40 percent improvement in 5-year survival rates for all cancers. Though this may sound great, Wark contends that it doesn't mean anything to the patients themselves. This is because such statistics don't specify whether the patient is alive and cancer free or alive and bedridden, on the verge of death. As long as they are alive within five years of diagnosis, they are all lumped together to make it seem as if the treatments are working.

Yet those patients who die within five years due to chemotoxicity or adverse drug reactions are never included in such statistics. Wark claims that cancer treatments aren't helping patients live longer; they are only helping to detect cancer sooner.

CHAPTER 7: THE BEAT CANCER MINDSET

Wark explains how he had to establish the right mindset in order to overcome his cancer. When you are terminally ill, you have to choose to live. The mindset you adopt will determine whether you survive or die. Wark describes five components that he has found in every cancer survivor he has met.

Key Takeaway: You are responsible for your cancer.

It is important for every cancer patient to admit the role they played in the development of their cancer. Wark argues that the choices you made in the past determine whether you get cancer or not. This is not meant to blame but to empower you to make better decisions. If you accept that your dict and lifestyle decisions are the cause of your cancer, then it means that you can do something to heal your body. However, if you live in denial, believing that cancer is genetic or bad luck, then you will feel powerless and become a victim of drugs and medical procedures.

Key Takeaway: Be willing to make sacrifices.

Wark explains how he was determined to eliminate everything in his life that was cancer-causing. He gave up junk foods, engaged in natural therapies, accepted his faults, prayed, and let go of all unforgiveness. He states that you must also change your thought patterns and think positively. If the doctor says you have a few months to live, reject those negative thoughts and do whatever it takes to live.

Key Takeaway: Take consistent, radical action.

You must be willing to do things that others consider crazy. If you make massive changes, you will get massive results. Wark believes that this is what successful survivors do. You have to go to great lengths to face your faults and fears and eliminate all disease promoters. This radical action should be a long-term goal rather than a magic bullet. Avoid the mentality of aiming for small changes and expecting great results. If you slacken off along the way, cancer will return.

Key Takeaway: Don't be afraid to make future plans.

When you make plans for your future, you are sending a signal that you expect to live a long life. Wark states that you should create future goals and document everything you are doing or want to achieve. Just three months after his diagnosis, he decided that he wanted to have children. This gave him a purpose and strengthened his will to live.

Key Takeaway: Don't forget to enjoy life.

Wark recounts how he learned to stay grateful and count his blessings every day. Cancer will make you fearful and steal your joy if you let it. You must choose to keep living a normal life and do the things that make you happy. Avoid looking back in anger at what you may have lost and simply enjoy the present moment.

CHAPTER 8: PLANTS VERSUS ZOMBIES

There are different types of foods that can help you fight cancer. Studies show that plants contain compounds that help prevent and reverse disease. Wark provides a list of fruits, vegetables, herbs, spices, and teas that stop cancer cells in their tracks. These anti-cancer compounds work to kill cancer cells, prevent their spread, or disrupt their metabolism.

Key Takeaway: Berries and lemons are the best anticancer fruits.

Wark contends that most fruits have some effect on cancer cells. Pineapples, peaches, bananas, apples, grapefruit, red grapes, and oranges may reduce cancer, but research shows that cranberries and lemons provide the strongest protection against cancer.

Cranberries can destroy 17 different types of cancer by protecting and repairing the damage caused by inflammation and oxidative stress. Raspberries, blackberries, and strawberries also stop cancer growth by up to 75 percent. The Indian gooseberry is high in antioxidants and vitamin C and can treat every known disease.

Key Takeaway: Vegetables from the allium and cruciferous family are potent cancer killers.

When researchers conducted experiments on cancer cells using 34 vegetable extracts, they discovered that many of the vegetables stopped cancer growth. However, vegetables from the allium family are the most powerful. These include garlic, leeks, green onions, and yellow onions. Garlic is so powerful that it should be consumed every day.

Cruciferous vegetables such as broccoli, kale, cauliflower, Brussels sprouts, and cabbage also stop cancer growth completely. Wark states that most of these anticancer vegetables form only 1 percent of the Western diet.

Key Takeaway: Turmeric, oregano, and cayenne pepper are the best anticancer spices.

According to Wark, India has a much lower cancer rate than Western nations because they consume a large number of spices. Research shows that the curcumin in turmeric kills many different types of cancer cells by triggering cell suicide. Oregano is an anticancer and antioxidant spice that contains the compound quercetin, which slows the growth and even kills cancer cells. Cayenne pepper contains capsaicin, which targets multiple cancer cells signals and suppresses tumors.

Key Takeaway: Some herbal teas are better at fighting cancer than others.

Though herbal teas are generally good for your health, Wark claims that some have greater anticancer properties than others. These include:

- Essiac Tea – Made from burdock root, rhubarb root, sheep sorrel, and slippery elm bark.

- Jason Winters Tea – A combination of chaparral, astralagus, and red clover.

- Dandelion Root Tea – Made from ground dandelion root steeped in hot water for 20 minutes.

- Green Tea – Matcha tea is the best type of green tea to heal cancer.

- Hibiscus Tea – It has more antioxidants than green tea and inhibits cancer cells from growing.

CHAPTER 9: HEROIC DOSES

Wark uses the example of the Daniel Fast to describe what an anti-cancer diet should look like. In the Bible, Daniel and his friends ate plant foods and water for 10 days, and by the end of it, they appeared healthier than the men who had been eating the king's fine foods.

Research shows that a diet consisting of fruits, vegetables, seeds, and nuts alone increases oxidative capacity and lowers oxidative stress and inflammation. Wark provides the three components of his anti-cancer diet—juicing, vegetable salads and fruit smoothies.

Key Takeaway: Plants are the key to beating cancer.

When Wark began his 90-day Daniel Fast, the first thing he did was to eliminate all animal products and processed foods from his diet. He stuck to whole, organic, plant foods. In one study, scientists were able to reverse prostate cancer by four percent by placing patients on a diet of low-fat, plant-based foods with stress management and daily exercise. The patients who didn't follow this regimen had a six percent increase in cancer progression.

The World Health Organization has categorized processed meats such as sausages and canned meat as Group 1 carcinogens. Research shows that animal products contain extremely high levels of methionine, an amino acid that cancer cells cannot survive without.

Key Takeaway: Juicing is better than chewing food.

Wark states that chewing fruits and vegetables is a form of juicing because you are splitting open cell walls and absorbing the nutrients. However, he argues that juicing is way more efficient for three reasons.

First, there is a limit to the amount of food you can chew in a day, but juicing allows you to consume a larger quantity of nutrients. Secondly, 90 percent of the nutrients in food are released when juicing, which is almost three times more than when chewing. Thirdly, a sick person uses a lot of energy when chewing food. With juicing, the patient's body easily absorbs the nutrients, thus conserving energy for fighting disease.

Key Takeaway: Fermented foods are good for your gut bacteria.

Maintaining a healthy gut is a crucial part of healing your body. Wark contends that fermented foods, which contain probiotic bacteria, will repopulate your microbiome and eliminate the disease-causing bacteria. This will strengthen your immunity and digestion. Foods such as kimchi, sauerkraut, and pickles are good examples. The only thing you have to watch out for is the salt content. Wark believes that too much sodium in kimchi and pickles is the reason for the high incidences of stomach cancer in Japan and Korea.

CHAPTER 10: BUILDING A NEW BODY

According to Wark, the food you eat will define the kind of body you have. Years of consuming unhealthy foods ultimately lead to a weakened body, but consuming whole foods allows your cells to regenerate over a short period of time. There are some herbs and spices are also crucial for providing your body with vital anti-cancer antioxidants. Wark takes a deep look at some foundational dietary principles that can help you maintain longevity and good health.

Key Takeaway: Moving closer to nature can help you beat cancer.

Wark describes how Stamatis Moraitis, a 66-year-old man who was diagnosed with lung cancer, managed to live to be 96 without any drugs, juicing, or alternative therapies. Moraitis simply decided to leave America and move back to his native Greek island of Ikaria. According to Wark, the Ikarians live a very social lifestyle, sharing whatever few resources they have. Theirs is a slow-paced life with little stress and long walks up and down the hills. They consume a lot of fresh local produce, plant foods, herbal teas, wild-caught fish, and very little meat or sugar. Though they drink a lot of coffee and wine, Ikarians are some of the healthiest and longest-living people.

Key Takeaway: Your poop indicates how healthy your body is.

When Dr. Denis Burkitt traveled to Africa as a medical missionary, he noticed that rural Africans didn't suffer from the chronic diseases that plagued industrialized nations. Apart from childhood diseases, their diet and lifestyle enabled them to live well beyond 100 years. However, what surprised Burkitt the most was the poop.

Food is supposed to pass out quickly from the bowels. If it stays too long, the poop releases toxins back into the body. Since Africans consume a diet rich in fiber and starch, food takes one and a half days to be eliminated. But for Westerners, it takes more than three whole days. Africans also poop twice a day and eliminate four times more poop daily than Europeans and Americans. Wark implies that the regularity and quality of poop is a good measure of a person's health.

CHAPTER 11: TAKE OUT THE TRASH

Your body comes into contact with so many toxins daily. This places a huge strain on your liver as your primary detoxification organ. However, Wark states that taking certain steps can minimize this toxic load and keep away disease. He examines some of the most common toxins that you need to be aware of and what you can do to protect yourself from unnecessary exposure.

Key Takeaway: Always check the label before buying.

Wark states that conventionally grown produce contains high levels of pesticides and herbicides. When buying fruits and vegetables, always pick organic ones, especially produce like apples, cucumbers, celery, peaches, cherry tomatoes, berries, and kale.

Check the label or sticker on every product to determine whether it is organic, GMO, or conventionally grown. Organic produce has a sticker with a five-digit code that starts with the number 9.

Key Takeaway: Avoid foods and products containing mercury and aluminum.

Though it's wise to avoid farm-bred fish because they contain excessive amounts of PCBs, Wark states that shellfish and wild fish also contain mercury. This is especially true for fish at the top of the food chain, such as shark, tuna, and king mackerel. The EPA classifies mercury as hazardous waste, yet the American Dental Association still recommends it to be used in silver amalgam fillings.

Aluminum is known to be a powerful neurotoxin that is linked to Alzheimer's. Yet most people don't realize that cheese has the highest quantity of aluminum. Manufacturers add sodium aluminum phosphate to enhance the flavor of cheese, but on the ingredients list, they refer to it simply as "salt." Canned meat also contains aluminum sulfate. Wark contends that the best solution is to stop using or consuming products containing these heavy metals so that your body can have time to eliminate them.

Key Takeaway: Clean up your air and your airwaves.

According to the EPA, there are more pollutants indoors than outdoors, such as mold spores, radon gas, and other volatile chemicals used in fabrics. Wark recommends that you get as much fresh air as possible while indoors by using air filters or houseplants such as lady palm, Boston fern, or peace lily.

You should also minimize electropollution in your home which is caused by all the electrical devices in your home. Do not live in houses located near power lines, use incandescent rather than fluorescent bulbs, and switch off your Wi-Fi at night. Studies show that overexposure to electromagnetic fields can be harmful. Wi-Fi radiation has been linked to male infertility, hormone disruption, and DNA damage.

Key Takeaway: You pay a heavy price for maintaining your beauty.

The beauty industry isn't as regulated as the food industry, yet your skin absorbs everything you apply onto it. Wark argues that some chemicals in makeup, lotions, deodorants, and oils are toxic. One study revealed that about half of personal care products contain carcinogens, with manufacturers rarely listing these toxins on the label. For example, mascara contains mercury, antiperspirants contain aluminum salts which contribute to breast cancer, and lipstick contains lead.

Some of the toxins you need to avoid in skin care products include:

- BHA – Used in fragrances but causes stomach cancer and liver damage

- Formaldehyde – Used to straighten hair and in cosmetics but is a neurotoxin and asthmagen

- Fragrances – Manufacturers aren't legally required to state the ingredients in their fragrances, but they contain chemicals that disrupt hormones

- Parabens – Used in conditioners and shampoos but cause developmental, reproductive, and endocrine disorders

- Retinol and retinyl products – Usually listed as Vitamin A compounds and used in makeup, lotions, and sunscreens. They are broken down by sunlight to release free radicals that cause skin tumors

CHAPTER 12: LET'S GET PHYSICAL

Wark takes a closer look at how exercise affects your health. He explains why staying physically active can reduce your risk of getting all kinds of diseases. Exercise helps the body detoxify and stay fit and healthy. Wark argues that any kind of body movement, including walking or even bouncing is good for you.

However, he stresses the importance of achieving a balance by engaging in the right amount of exercise. Proper rest and sleep are also vital for the detoxification process. Any kind of body movement that you engage in daily for 30 to 60 minutes, especially if you are recovering from treatment, will improve the quality of your life.

Key Takeaway: Too much exercise is bad for your health.

Most Americans live a sedentary lifestyle where they spend more than 97 percent of their time sitting. This explains why the US has the shortest lifespan in the industrialized world. However, Wark contends that professional athletes have a shorter life expectancy than the average American. This is due to extreme weight and endurance exercise.

When you exercise too much for too long, your body produces high levels of free radicals, cortisol, and adrenaline. This leads to suppressed immunity, cell damage, and inflammation. This puts you at greater risk of disease.

Key Takeaway: Jumping on a trampoline helps your lymphatic system detoxify your body.

Since you cannot avoid toxins entirely, Wark states that detoxifying your lymphatic system is a crucial process. Your lymphatic system produces white blood cells and also carries away metabolic waste for elimination via the excretory organs. However, unlike blood, lymphatic fluid doesn't have a pump to ensure continuous circulation. The only way your lymphatic fluid can flow is via body movement.

Wark suggests recommends "rebounding" as a way to help stimulate the circulation of the lymphatic system. This involves jumping on a mini-trampoline. It is low-impact, improves strength, triggers sweating, and stresses every cell in your body at once.

Key Takeaway: The sun can protect you from cancer.

Most people believe that exposure to the sun raises the chances of developing skin cancers. However, only 2,000 people die from skin cancer per year. Studies show that getting more sunshine can prevent other cancers that are far more deadly, including colon and breast cancer, which kill about 138,000 people annually. Vitamin D is critical for preventing cancer.

CHAPTER 13: UNDER PRESSURE

Wark describes how stressed out his lifestyle was right after college. He was preparing for a wedding that was only a few months away and had to find a decent job. When he was hired by a financial firm, he worked on a commission basis, and he was constantly worried about finding new clients and keeping his job.

After he began investing in his passion, rental properties, he was still stressed out. He was now working two jobs and surviving on fast food, sugar, and caffeine. One year later, he was diagnosed with cancer. According to Wark, stress is the common denominator in every cancer patient he has ever counseled.

Key Takeaway: Stress deactivates your immune system.

Whenever you are under stress, your body automatically goes into survival mode. It begins when certain senses are triggered and you experience specific thoughts and emotions. If you feel fearful, that emotion causes adrenalin and cortisol to be released. Almost immediately, all energy is diverted away from vital functions toward your muscles.

According to Wark, this is why you can't think straight or remember your answers during a test. Every time stress hormones are released, your immune system is turned off to conserve energy. Your digestive and reproductive systems are also switched off. This is a good thing in the short-term, but if it persists for too long, you become vulnerable to diseases that you normally would have fought off.

Key Takeaway: Stress is a good thing, but chronic stress is a killer.

Chronic stress means experiencing stressful events every day. Wark describes it as being stalked by a tiger daily and thus you cannot afford to stop running. This is what most people experience in the modern world, thanks to financial, family, work, and social demands. Toss in poor sleeping habits, extreme exercise, and stimulants and things get worse.

Some of the major side effects of chronic stress include:

- Chronic fatigue

- Stress eating which leads to excess glucose and inflammation

- Crohn's disease

- Immune suppression which can lead to cancer

- Reduced brain function

Studies show that anti-cancer drugs are ineffective in mice under stress. According to one cancer expert, "Stress sends a signal into the cancer that allows tumor cells to escape from the cancer and spread through the body."

Key Takeaway: Be proactive in relieving stress.

According to Wark, the most important step in reducing stress is eliminating worry. He bases his advice on the Bible, where Jesus told his disciples not to worry about their daily needs but to put their faith in Him. For Wark, prayer and faith in God helped him overcome worry and doubt.

Wark recommends that you look at every single problem in your life and take action on it. Make a list with two columns – Problems/Stressors and Solutions. If a problem is within your control, deal with it directly. If it is not, leave it to God. Laughing and singing lower stress and are also good for your immune system.

CHAPTER 14: SPIRITUAL HEALING

Wark explains how cancer forced his faith in God to grow. Though he didn't understand why God allowed this to happen to him, he chose to trust that something good would come out of his cancer diagnosis. Through his ordeal, Wark learned about the importance of spiritual healing in overcoming cancer. He argues that you must first allow God to heal your heart before your body does is restored. You must set aside your doubt, bitterness, and other negative feelings and forgive everyone, including yourself.

Key Takeaway: You must think positively to beat cancer.

Your reality is a product of your thoughts and beliefs. Wark believes that this is a powerful concept that can help every cancer patient. He claims that those patients who believe that their treatment is going to work end up defying the odds, while those who don't have faith in a particular therapy end up succumbing.

Positive affirmations have a lot of power because they encourage you and change the way you feel or see yourself. You must avoid negative self-talk and criticism. Wark argues that you should also talk to your organs and command them to be healed. For him, meditating on healing scriptures daily helped him speak healing into his body.

Key Takeaway: Put your faith in God.

When you become sick, society expects you to put your faith in doctors. This is often a fear-based decision. However, Wark states that you must first make a faith-based decision by trusting in God. During prayer, don't just ask God to show you what to do. Ask him to also show you the changes to make in your life. Then wait for an answer and make the right changes.

Key Takeaway: Guard your heart against bitterness and resentment.

According to Wark, three of the worst emotional states are bitterness, unforgiveness, and resentment. It is important to allow your heart to heal from past trauma by forgiving everyone who has caused you pain. Go into prayer and try to remember all those who have wronged you in the past. Then pray for them and bless them. This is difficult for most people to do but it is very important because any kind of bitterness will block your healing.

Wark had to do this himself because he realized that God can only heal you after He has healed your heart. If you don't forgive others, then God cannot forgive and heal you. In life, everyone reaps what they have sown. If someone did something to offend you, rest assured that they will get what they deserve. However, you must release your heart from the bitterness by letting it all go.

EDITORIAL REVIEW

In his book *Chris Beat Cancer: A Comprehensive Plan for Healing Naturally*, Chris Wark argues that the cancer industry has been taking cancer patients for a ride. Chris states that the medical-industrial complex, comprising oncologists, cancer clinics, and pharmaceutical companies, is only interested in making billions of dollars in profits instead of actually treating patients. He claims that the cancer industry has forsaken the Hippocratic principle to "First do no harm."

When Chris is diagnosed with colorectal cancer in 2003, he initially goes along with the doctor's recommendations. He is convinced by doctors that stomach surgery and chemotherapy are the only options he has to stay alive. But after his surgery, he has a change of heart. After much prayer, Chris believes that God is leading him down a different path that doesn't involve conventional medicine. When he receives a book about a man who healed himself of cancer by eating raw plant foods and juicing, Chris feels encouraged to reject chemotherapy and clean up his diet and lifestyle instead. Today, 15 years later, Chris claims to be cancer-free and is inspiring others to follow a similar naturopathic diet.

In his book, he does a good job of providing stacks of statistics and scientific evidence to prove his position. He is not a scientist or doctor, so the writing isn't academic. However, he ensures that his information is well-researched. He does well in describing his diet, which includes fruits, vegetables, and lots of herbs and spices that are potent antioxidants.

The tone of the book is relatively casual. Chris doesn't appear to be interested in sounding smart when providing scientific evidence and data from research studies. He comes across as a regular guy who learned a few things about cancer the hard way.

At some point, the book may feel depressing because he implies that everything you buy, touch, or breathe is contaminated. If everything is toxic, including the paint in your house, where are you supposed to go? However, Chris does remind everyone that strengthening their immune system through diet and lifestyle change is the best option. If you can avoid foods containing toxic chemicals and incorporate plant foods, herbs, and spices into your daily diet, you can heal your body of any disease.

It is important to note that Chris prioritizes acquiring the right mindset and belief system before even doing any of the alternative therapies he has provided. If you get caught up in feeling sorry for yourself or refusing to take full responsibility for your condition, you won't beat cancer.

Are there other books out there that cover cancer in a similar perspective? Absolutely! If you have been reading up on anti-cancer literature lately, you won't find anything new in this book. Chris has been influenced by many other authors and alternative therapy gurus, such as George Malkamus, Dr. Max Gerson, and Ty Bollinger. The only difference is the personal journey in the book.

Chris Beat Cancer hits hard against the cancer industry and highlights the financial and moral corruption within it, but it isn't necessarily an eye-opener. It is a great read though, especially if you aren't familiar with how the cancer industry works. At the end of the day, Chris states that he isn't trying to bring down the medical establishment. All he wants is for people to make informed decisions instead of going along with whatever their doctor tells them.

BACKGROUND ON AUTHOR

Chris Wark is an American author, blogger, wellness crusader, speaker, and patient advocate. In 2003, Chris was diagnosed with stage III colorectal cancer at 26 years old. After surgery, he rejected chemotherapy and instead chose to change his diet and lifestyle. After successfully healing his body of cancer using natural therapies, Chris became a personal health advocate. Today he inspires people all over the world to use nutrition to reverse disease and improve their health.

Chris attended the University of Memphis and graduated in 2001 with a bachelor's degree in Business Administration-Marketing/Management. He briefly worked for a financial planning firm before venturing into real estate investing in 2002. He is still a real estate investor to date and is involved in acquiring, renovating, managing, and selling residential and commercial properties.

He is also the curator of the health blog *chrisbeatcancer.com*, a website that features articles about scientific and natural/nutritional therapies. The website has had millions of page views and more than 100,000 subscribers. Chris is also a health/wellness cancer consultant who offers one-on-one coaching. He has been featured on numerous TV and radio shows, including the award-winning films *The C Word, The Truth About Cancer,* and many others. He has also been a featured presenter in several health conferences, including *Cure to Cancer Conference* and *Healing Cancer World Summit.*

Chris lives in Tennessee with his wife, Micah and their two daughters Marin and Mackenzie. *Chris Beat Cancer* is his first book.

END OF BOOK SUMMARY

*If you enjoyed this **ZIP Reads** publication, we encourage you to purchase a copy of the original book.*

We'd also love an honest review on Amazon.com!

Want **FREE** book summaries delivered weekly? Sign up for our email list and get notified of all our new releases, free promos, and $0.99 deals!

No spam, just books.

Sign up at http://zipreads.co

ZIPREADS

Made in the USA
Coppell, TX
01 February 2024